GRACE
FOR THE PACE

FINDING GOD'S STRENGTH
FOR YOUR DAILY RACE

PAUL CHAPPELL

First published in 2010 by Striving Together Publications, a ministry of Lancaster Baptist Church, Lancaster, CA 93535. Striving Together Publications is committed to providing tried, trusted, and proven books that will further equip local churches to carry out the Great Commission. Your comments and suggestions are valued.

Striving Together Publications
4020 E. Lancaster Blvd.
Lancaster, CA 93535
800.201.7748

Cover design by Andrew Jones
Layout by Craig Parker
Edited by Robert Byers, Rebekah Hanks, Tina Butterfield
Special thanks to our proofreaders.

ISBN 978-1-59894-098-5
Printed in the United States of America

Table of Contents

A Renewing Grace

Text

MARK 16:1–11

1   *And when the sabbath was past, Mary Magdalene, and Mary the mother of James, and Salome, had bought sweet spices, that they might come and anoint him.*

2   *And very early in the morning the first day of the week, they came unto the sepulchre at the rising of the sun.*

3   *And they said among themselves, Who shall roll us away the stone from the door of the sepulchre?*

4   *And when they looked, they saw that the stone was rolled away: for it was very great.*

5   *And entering into the sepulchre, they saw a young man sitting on the right side, clothed in a long white garment; and they were affrighted.*

6   *And he saith unto them, Be not affrighted: Ye seek Jesus of Nazareth, which was crucified: he is risen; he is not here: behold the place where they laid him.*

7   *But go your way, tell his disciples and Peter that he goeth before you into Galilee: there shall ye see him, as he said unto you.*

8   *And they went out quickly, and fled from the sepulchre; for they trembled and were amazed: neither said they any thing to any man; for they were afraid.*

9   *Now when Jesus was risen early the first day of the week, he appeared first to Mary Magdalene, out of whom he had cast seven devils.*

10   *And she went and told them that had been with him, as they mourned and wept.*

11   *And they, when they had heard that he was alive, and had been seen of her, believed not.*

Overview

Grace has many facets: it provides our salvation, healing, hope, and purpose in life. We see grace illustrated vividly in the Resurrection. Grace transformed Mary's pain into hope, replaced the disciples' pessimism with faith, and gave their lives new purpose and meaning.

Many Christians have not yet come to understand the role grace plays in their daily walk with God, and as a result, they are living below their privileges as children of God. While the Resurrection is a true historical event, its impact is not exclusive to first century Christians; rather, God extends to today's Christian the grace to live a victorious Christian life through the power of Christ's Resurrection.

Introduction

_____

_____

_____

I. Renewed from _____

A. Through _____ in Christ

EPHESIANS 2:8

8   For by grace are ye saved through faith; and that not of yourselves: it is the gift of God:

PSALM 103:12

12   As far as the east is from the west, so far hath he removed our transgressions from us.

B. Through the _____ of Christ

1 CORINTHIANS 15:19–20

19   If in this life only we have hope in Christ, we are of all men most miserable.

20   But now is Christ risen from the dead, and become the firstfruits of them that slept.

II. Renewed from _____

A. Pessimism because of _____

B. Pessimism because of _____

JOHN 14:3

3   And if I go and prepare a place for you, I will come again, and receive you unto myself; that where I am, there ye may be also.

MATTHEW 12:40

40 *For as Jonas was three days and three nights in the whale's belly; so shall the Son of man be three days and three nights in the heart of the earth.*

JOHN 2:19

19 *Jesus answered and said unto them, Destroy this temple, and in three days I will raise it up.*

JOHN 20:18–20

18 *Mary Magdalene came and told the disciples that she had seen the Lord, and that he had spoken these things unto her.*

19 *Then the same day at evening, being the first day of the week, when the doors were shut where the disciples were assembled for fear of the Jews, came Jesus and stood in the midst, and saith unto them, Peace be unto you.*

20 *And when he had so said, he shewed unto them his hands and his side. Then were the disciples glad, when they saw the Lord.*

III. Renewed for a _____

MATTHEW 28:16–20

16 *Then the eleven disciples went away into Galilee, into a mountain where Jesus had appointed them.*

17 *And when they saw him, they worshipped him: but some doubted.*

18 *And Jesus came and spake unto them, saying, All power is given unto me in heaven and in earth.*

19 *Go ye therefore, and teach all nations, baptizing them in the name of the Father, and of the Son, and of the Holy Ghost:*

20   Teaching them to observe all things whatsoever I have commanded you: and, lo, I am with you alway, even unto the end of the world. Amen.

A. *To share in the gift of His* _____
2 PETER 3:9
9   The Lord is not slack concerning his promise, as some men count slackness; but is longsuffering to us-ward, not willing that any should perish, but that all should come to repentance.

1 CORINTHIANS 15:3–4
3   For I delivered unto you first of all that which I also received, how that Christ died for our sins according to the scriptures;
4   And that he was buried, and that he rose again the third day according to the scriptures:

B. *To share His* _____
JOHN 20:21
21   Then said Jesus to them again, Peace be unto you: as my Father hath sent me, even so send I you.

Conclusion

_____

_____

_____

Study Questions

1. How did you come to realize that you needed God's grace in your life?

2. Through what means does God's grace renew us from pain?

3. How does the Resurrection give us hope for the future?

4. Why do you think so many people are pessimists today?

5. In what areas are you tempted to doubt the promises of God?

6. What are the purposes God has in offering you grace?

7. Whom do you know that needs to hear the Gospel?

8. How can you demonstrate your appreciation for the grace of God?

Memory Verses

Ephesians 2:4–5

4 But God, who is rich in mercy, for his great love wherewith he loved us,

5 Even when we were dead in sins, hath quickened us together with Christ, (by grace ye are saved;)

God's
riches
at
Ch
E

A Restoring Grace

Text

JOHN 18:25–27

25 And Simon Peter stood and warmed himself. They said therefore unto him, Art not thou also one of his disciples? He denied it, and said, I am not.

26 One of the servants of the high priest, being his kinsman whose ear Peter cut off, saith, Did not I see thee in the garden with him?

27 Peter then denied again: and immediately the cock crew.

Overview

Every child of God receives the Holy Spirit at the moment of salvation, and His full power and influence immediately become available to the believer. Though converted, Christians are not necessarily free from old patterns of worldly thoughts and actions. Sinful desires still remain.

If Christians are not careful, we can easily fall back into old habits, allowing those habits to take over and govern our actions and reactions. Fleshly patterns of decision-making always lead to consequences. When we sin, we need the restoring grace of God to bring us back into fellowship with Him. By properly responding to that grace, we will be renewed for His service.

Introduction

_____

_____

_____

I. Peter's _____

A. *He was _____.*

PROVERBS 16:18

18 Pride goeth before destruction, and an haughty spirit before a fall.

1. PETER THOUGHT HE WAS STRONGER THAN OTHERS.

JOHN 13:36–38

36 Simon Peter said unto him, Lord, whither goest thou? Jesus answered him, Whither I go, thou canst not follow me now; but thou shalt follow me afterwards.

37 Peter said unto him, Lord, why cannot I follow thee now? I will lay down my life for thy sake.

38 Jesus answered him, Wilt thou lay down thy life for my sake? Verily, verily, I say unto thee, The cock shall not crow, till thou hast denied me thrice.

2. PETER UNDERESTIMATED THE PERSISTENCE OF SATAN.

LUKE 22:31–34

31 And the Lord said, Simon, Simon, behold, Satan hath desired to have you, that he may sift you as wheat:

32 But I have prayed for thee, that thy faith fail not: and when thou art converted, strengthen thy brethren.

33   And he said unto him, Lord, I am ready to go with thee, both into prison, and to death.

34   And he said, I tell thee, Peter, the cock shall not crow this day, before that thou shalt thrice deny that thou knowest me.

B.   He was _____.

MATTHEW 26:34–36, 39–41

34   Jesus said unto him, Verily I say unto thee, That this night, before the cock crow, thou shalt deny me thrice.

35   Peter said unto him, Though I should die with thee, yet will I not deny thee. Likewise also said all the disciples.

36   Then cometh Jesus with them unto a place called Gethsemane, and saith unto the disciples, Sit ye here, while I go and pray yonder.

39   And he went a little farther, and fell on his face, and prayed, saying, O my Father, if it be possible, let this cup pass from me: nevertheless not as I will, but as thou wilt.

40   And he cometh unto the disciples, and findeth them asleep, and saith unto Peter, What, could ye not watch with me one hour?

41   Watch and pray, that ye enter not into temptation: the spirit indeed is willing, but the flesh is weak.

C.   He was _____.

LUKE 22:54–62

54   Then took they him, and led him, and brought him into the high priest's house. And Peter followed afar off.

55   And when they had kindled a fire in the midst of the hall, and were set down together, Peter sat down among them.

56   But a certain maid beheld him as he sat by the fire, and earnestly looked upon him, and said, This man was also with him.

57   And he denied him, saying, Woman, I know him not.

58   And after a little while another saw him, and said, Thou art also of them. And Peter said, Man, I am not.

59   And about the space of one hour after another confidently affirmed, saying, Of a truth this fellow also was with him: for he is a Galilaean.

60   And Peter said, Man, I know not what thou sayest. And immediately, while he yet spake, the cock crew.

61   And the Lord turned, and looked upon Peter. And Peter remembered the word of the Lord, how he had said unto him, Before the cock crow, thou shalt deny me thrice.

62   And Peter went out, and wept bitterly.

II. Peter's _____

JOHN 21:3

3   Simon Peter saith unto them, I go a fishing. They say unto him, We also go with thee. They went forth, and entered into a ship immediately: and that night they caught nothing.

A. *Jesus* _____ *to him.*

JOHN 21:12–17

12 *Jesus saith unto them, Come and dine. And one of the disciples durst ask him, Who art thou? knowing that it was the Lord.*

13 *Jesus then cometh, and taketh bread, and giveth them, and fish likewise.*

14 *This is now the third time that Jesus shewed himself to his disciples, after that he was risen from the dead.*

15 *So when they had dined, Jesus saith to Simon Peter, Simon, son of Jonas, lovest thou me more than these? He saith unto him, Yea, Lord; thou knowest that I love thee. He saith unto him, Feed my lambs.*

16 *He saith to him again the second time, Simon, son of Jonas, lovest thou me? He saith unto him, Yea, Lord; thou knowest that I love thee. He saith unto him, Feed my sheep.*

17 *He saith unto him the third time, Simon, son of Jonas, lovest thou me? Peter was grieved because he said unto him the third time, Lovest thou me? And he said unto him, Lord, thou knowest all things; thou knowest that I love thee. Jesus saith unto him, Feed my sheep.*

B. *The Holy Spirit* _____ *him.*

JOHN 14:16–17

16 *And I will pray the Father, and he shall give you another Comforter, that he may abide with you for ever;*

17 *Even the Spirit of truth; whom the world cannot receive, because it seeth him not, neither knoweth*

him: but ye know him; for he dwelleth with you, and shall be in you.

ACTS 1:8

8   *But ye shall receive power, after that the Holy Ghost is come upon you: and ye shall be witnesses unto me both in Jerusalem, and in all Judaea, and in Samaria, and unto the uttermost part of the earth.*

III. Peter's _____

A. *Peter preached the _____ of Christ.*
ACTS 2:38–41

38   Then Peter said unto them, Repent, and be baptized every one of you in the name of Jesus Christ for the remission of sins, and ye shall receive the gift of the Holy Ghost.

39   For the promise is unto you, and to your children, and to all that are afar off, even as many as the Lord our God shall call.

40   And with many other words did he testify and exhort, saying, Save yourselves from this untoward generation.

41   Then they that gladly received his word were baptized: and the same day there were added unto them about three thousand souls.

B. *Peter proclaimed the _____ of Christ.*
ACTS 4:8–12

8   Then Peter, filled with the Holy Ghost, said unto them, Ye rulers of the people, and elders of Israel,

9   If we this day be examined of the good deed done to the impotent man, by what means he is made whole;

10   Be it known unto you all, and to all the people of Israel, that by the name of Jesus Christ of Nazareth, whom ye crucified, whom God raised from the dead, even by him doth this man stand here before you whole.

11   This is the stone which was set at nought of you builders, which is become the head of the corner.

12   Neither is there salvation in any other: for there is none other name under heaven given among men, whereby we must be saved.

Conclusion

_____

_____

_____

Study Questions

1. What are some areas in which you return to fleshly patterns of behavior?

2. What were the three causes of Peter's failure?

3. How does pride manifest itself in your life?

4. What took place that brought about Peter's restoration?

5. What indicated the power of the Spirit was on Peter's life?

6. How did Peter respond to his restoration?

7. What are some ways in which you are serving God today?

8. How has God's grace restored your life?

Memory Verses

JAMES 4:6–8

6   But he giveth more grace. Wherefore he saith, God resisteth the proud, but giveth grace unto the humble.

7   Submit yourselves therefore to God. Resist the devil, and he will flee from you.

8   Draw nigh to God, and he will draw nigh to you. Cleanse your hands, ye sinners; and purify your hearts, ye double minded.

A Replenishing Grace

Text

2 TIMOTHY 2:1–3

1   *Thou therefore, my son, be strong in the grace that is in Christ Jesus.*

2   *And the things that thou hast heard of me among many witnesses, the same commit thou to faithful men, who shall be able to teach others also.*

3   *Thou therefore endure hardness, as a good soldier of Jesus Christ.*

Overview

Every Christian is living in the middle of a battlefield. Just as soldiers on the frontlines of war need time away for "R&R" (rest and recreation), we also need our strength replenished for the spiritual warfare we face. Our hectic lives sometimes make us feel like we're stuck in the spin cycle of a washing machine. That's where grace comes in.

Fighting the battle in our own strength is impossible. Spiritual muscles, like physical muscles, are only developed through effort and struggle. No one ever became a strong soldier for Christ without going through training. God's training program includes deploying His grace to help in preparing us to win the victory.

Introduction

_____

_____

_____

I.   His Grace Replenishes Our _____

A. *Strength for* _____
HEBREWS 12:28
28 Wherefore we receiving a kingdom which cannot be moved, let us have grace, whereby we may serve God acceptably with reverence and godly fear:

B. *Strength for* _____
JAMES 5:10
10 Take, my brethren, the prophets, who have spoken in the name of the Lord, for an example of suffering affliction, and of patience.

1. WHEN WE ARE FEARFUL
2 TIMOTHY 1:7
7 For God hath not given us the spirit of fear; but of power, and of love, and of a sound mind.

2. WHEN WE ARE WEARY
2 CORINTHIANS 4:16
16 For which cause we faint not; but though our outward man perish, yet the inward man is renewed day by day.

II. His Grace Replenishes Our _____

A. From _____ to _____

PHILEMON 18–19, 25

18   If he hath wronged thee, or oweth thee ought, put that on mine account;

19   I Paul have written it with mine own hand, I will repay it: albeit I do not say to thee how thou owest unto me even thine own self besides.

25   The grace of our Lord Jesus Christ be with your spirit. Amen.

2 TIMOTHY 4:22

22   The Lord Jesus Christ be with thy spirit. Grace be with you. Amen.

B. From _____ to _____

2 THESSALONIANS 2:16–17

16   Now our Lord Jesus Christ himself, and God, even our Father, which hath loved us, and hath given us everlasting consolation and good hope through grace,

17   Comfort your hearts, and stablish you in every good word and work.

III. His Grace Replenishes Our _____

A. God supplies _____ by His grace.

EPHESIANS 2:8–9

8   For by grace are ye saved through faith; and that not of yourselves: it is the gift of God:

9   Not of works, lest any man should boast.

B. *God supplies* _____ *by His grace.*

HEBREWS 4:15–16

15 *For we have not an high priest which cannot be touched with the feeling of our infirmities; but was in all points tempted like as we are, yet without sin.*

16 *Let us therefore come boldly unto the throne of grace, that we may obtain mercy, and find grace to help in time of need.*

Conclusion

_____

_____

_____

Study Questions

1. In what ways do you find yourself involved in spiritual warfare?

2. In what two areas does God's grace give us strength?

3. How has suffering helped you grow in your Christian life?

4. In what two areas does grace replenish our spirit?

5. When has grace brought comfort to your life?

6. What does God provide for us through His grace?

7. What are you doing to stay strong in spiritual warfare?

8. What struggle has God allowed in your life to make you stronger?

Memory Verses

HEBREWS 4:15–16

15 *For we have not an high priest which cannot be touched with the feeling of our infirmities; but was in all points tempted like as we are, yet without sin.*

16 *Let us therefore come boldly unto the throne of grace, that we may obtain mercy, and find grace to help in time of need.*

A Resting Grace

Text

1 PETER 5:10–12

10 But the God of all grace, who hath called us unto his eternal glory by Christ Jesus, after that ye have suffered a while, make you perfect, stablish, strengthen, settle you.

11 To him be glory and dominion for ever and ever. Amen.

12 By Silvanus, a faithful brother unto you, as I suppose, I have written briefly, exhorting, and testifying that this is the true grace of God wherein ye stand.

Overview

God designed the Christian life to move from grace to grace. We are saved by grace, but we also need sanctifying grace, serving grace, and sacrificing grace. Grace is especially important for times of suffering. In any difficulty, grace is a dependable foundation on which we can rest.

Grace strengthens and settles our faith so we can survive the storms of life. It is the source of our hope during trials, leading us to view the Word of God properly, as the foundation for our stability. God leads us through trials with the goal of building and strengthening our faith through His grace, and we must learn to view problems in light of this divine purpose.

Introduction

_____

_____

_____

I. Grace for _____

A. _____ *attacks*

JAMES 4:7

7   *Submit yourselves therefore to God. Resist the devil, and he will flee from you.*

2 CORINTHIANS 12:7–9

7   *And lest I should be exalted above measure through the abundance of the revelations, there was given to me a thorn in the flesh, the messenger of Satan to buffet me, lest I should be exalted above measure.*

8   *For this thing I besought the Lord thrice, that it might depart from me.*

9   *And he said unto me, My grace is sufficient for thee: for my strength is made perfect in weakness. Most gladly therefore will I rather glory in my infirmities, that the power of Christ may rest upon me.*

B. _____ *afflictions*

1 CORINTHIANS 10:13

13   *There hath no temptation taken you but such as is common to man: but God is faithful, who will not suffer you to be tempted above that ye are able; but will with the temptation also make a way to escape, that ye may be able to bear it.*

1 PETER 1:6–7

6   Wherein ye greatly rejoice, though now for a season, if need be, ye are in heaviness through manifold temptations:

7   That the trial of your faith, being much more precious than of gold that perisheth, though it be tried with fire, might be found unto praise and honour and glory at the appearing of Jesus Christ:

II. Grace for _____

A. The _____ of our faith

B. The _____ of our faith

2 THESSALONIANS 2:16–17

16   Now our Lord Jesus Christ himself, and God, even our Father, which hath loved us, and hath given us everlasting consolation and good hope through grace,

17   Comfort your hearts, and stablish you in every good word and work.

C. The _____ of our faith

1. HE HAS POWER TO STRENGTHEN US.

PHILIPPIANS 4:13

13   I can do all things through Christ which strengtheneth me.

2. HE HAS A PURPOSE IN STRENGTHENING US.

LUKE 22:32

32   But I have prayed for thee, that thy faith fail not: and when thou art converted, strengthen thy brethren.

III. Grace for _____

A. Settled on a _____

1. GOD'S WORD IS OUR FOUNDATION.

MATTHEW 7:24–27

24 *Therefore whosoever heareth these sayings of mine, and doeth them, I will liken him unto a wise man, which built his house upon a rock:*

25 *And the rain descended, and the floods came, and the winds blew, and beat upon that house; and it fell not: for it was founded upon a rock.*

26 *And every one that heareth these sayings of mine, and doeth them not, shall be likened unto a foolish man, which built his house upon the sand:*

27 *And the rain descended, and the floods came, and the winds blew, and beat upon that house; and it fell: and great was the fall of it.*

2. GOD'S WORD IS OUR STABILIZATION.

EPHESIANS 4:11–15

11 *And he gave some, apostles; and some, prophets; and some, evangelists; and some, pastors and teachers;*

12 *For the perfecting of the saints, for the work of the ministry, for the edifying of the body of Christ:*

13 *Till we all come in the unity of the faith, and of the knowledge of the Son of God, unto a perfect man, unto the measure of the stature of the fulness of Christ:*

14 *That we henceforth be no more children, tossed to and fro, and carried about with every wind of doctrine by the sleight of men, and cunning craftiness, whereby they lie in wait to deceive;*

15 But speaking the truth in love, may grow up into him in all things, which is the head, even Christ:

B. Settled on a _____

1 CORINTHIANS 3:11

11 For other foundation can no man lay than that is laid, which is Jesus Christ.

MATTHEW 16:17–18

17 And Jesus answered and said unto him, Blessed art thou, Simon Barjona: for flesh and blood hath not revealed it unto thee, but my Father which is in heaven.

18 And I say also unto thee, That thou art Peter, and upon this rock I will build my church; and the gates of hell shall not prevail against it.

1 CORINTHIANS 10:4

4 And did all drink the same spiritual drink: for they drank of that spiritual Rock that followed them: and that Rock was Christ.

Conclusion

_____

_____

_____

Study Questions

1. In what two types of suffering does grace help us?

2. How has grace helped you deal with affliction in your life?

3. In what three ways does grace help our faith?

4. What two truths did we learn about God's strengthening of our faith?

5. In what ways is your faith stronger now than it was when you were saved?

6. How does grace settle us as believers?

7. What two things does the Bible provide for our faith?

8. When have you used a verse or passage from the Bible to keep you on track?

Memory Verses

2 CORINTHIANS 12:7–9

7   And lest I should be exalted above measure through the abundance of the revelations, there was given to me a thorn in the flesh, the messenger of Satan to buffet me, lest I should be exalted above measure.

8   For this thing I besought the Lord thrice, that it might depart from me.

9   And he said unto me, My grace is sufficient for thee: for my strength is made perfect in weakness. Most gladly therefore will I rather glory in my infirmities, that the power of Christ may rest upon me.

A Redeeming Grace

Text

EPHESIANS 2:1–9

1   And you hath he quickened, who were dead in trespasses and sins;

2   Wherein in time past ye walked according to the course of this world, according to the prince of the power of the air, the spirit that now worketh in the children of disobedience:

3   Among whom also we all had our conversation in times past in the lusts of our flesh, fulfilling the desires of the flesh and of the mind; and were by nature the children of wrath, even as others.

4   But God, who is rich in mercy, for his great love wherewith he loved us,

5   Even when we were dead in sins, hath quickened us together with Christ, (by grace ye are saved;)

6   And hath raised us up together, and made us sit together in heavenly places in Christ Jesus:

7   That in the ages to come he might shew the exceeding riches of his grace in his kindness toward us through Christ Jesus.

8   For by grace are ye saved through faith; and that not of yourselves: it is the gift of God:

9   Not of works, lest any man should boast.

Overview

God has a heart of grace and love for every one of us. If He did not, we would all be in Hell, which is what we deserve. But grace provides the means for our salvation and a way to join God in Heaven for eternity.

Often, when people have been saved for a number of years, they take that grace for granted and lose their appreciation for it. In this lesson, we will look at the glory of God's grace and focus on how much that grace cost Jesus Christ. Then we'll look at the power of His grace, and finally we'll see how we can partake of the riches of grace that are freely offered to us.

Introduction

_____

_____

_____

I. The _____ of Grace

EPHESIANS 2:4–5

4 But God, who is rich in mercy, for his great love wherewith he loved us,

5 Even when we were dead in sins, hath quickened us together with Christ, (by grace ye are saved;)

A. *A payment of Christ's* _____

JOHN 3:16

16 For God so loved the world, that he gave his only begotten Son, that whosoever believeth in him should not perish, but have everlasting life.

ROMANS 5:8

8 But God commendeth his love toward us, in that, while we were yet sinners, Christ died for us.

B. *A payment of Christ's* _____

1 PETER 1:18–19

18 Forasmuch as ye know that ye were not redeemed with corruptible things, as silver and gold, from your vain conversation received by tradition from your fathers;

19 But with the precious blood of Christ, as of a lamb without blemish and without spot:

Romans 3:23–25

23 *For all have sinned, and come short of the glory of God;*

24 *Being justified freely by his grace through the redemption that is in Christ Jesus:*

25 *Whom God hath set forth to be a propitiation through faith in his blood, to declare his righteousness for the remission of sins that are past, through the forbearance of God;*

II. The _____ of Grace

Ephesians 2:8

8 For by grace are ye saved through faith; and that not of yourselves: it is the gift of God:

A. *Power to* _____ *us*

Romans 3:24

24 *Being justified freely by his grace through the redemption that is in Christ Jesus:*

Ephesians 1:7

7 *In whom we have redemption through his blood, the forgiveness of sins, according to the riches of his grace;*

B. *Power to* _____ *us*

Romans 3:24–25

24 *Being justified freely by his grace through the redemption that is in Christ Jesus:*

25 *Whom God hath set forth to be a propitiation through faith in his blood, to declare his righteousness*

for the remission of sins that are past, through the forbearance of God;

C. Power to _____ us

TITUS 2:11–13

11 *For the grace of God that bringeth salvation hath appeared to all men,*

12 *Teaching us that, denying ungodliness and worldly lusts, we should live soberly, righteously, and godly, in this present world;*

13 *Looking for that blessed hope, and the glorious appearing of the great God and our Saviour Jesus Christ;*

III. The _____ of Grace

EPHESIANS 2:8–9

8 *For by grace are ye saved through faith; and that not of yourselves: it is the gift of God:*

9 *Not of works, lest any man should boast.*

A. By faith in Christ's _____

TITUS 3:4–7

4 *But after that the kindness and love of God our Saviour toward man appeared,*

5 *Not by works of righteousness which we have done, but according to his mercy he saved us, by the washing of regeneration, and renewing of the Holy Ghost;*

6 *Which he shed on us abundantly through Jesus Christ our Saviour;*

7 *That being justified by his grace, we should be made heirs according to the hope of eternal life.*

41

B. *By faith in Christ's work* _____
ROMANS 11:6

6 *And if by grace, then is it no more of works: otherwise grace is no more grace. But if it be of works, then is it no more grace: otherwise work is no more work.*

Conclusion

_____

_____

_____

Study Questions

1. How was the payment for grace made on our behalf?

2. How did you first learn about God's grace?

3. How is the power of grace demonstrated?

4. What does it mean to be redeemed?

5. What lessons have you learned from grace in your life?

6. How do we partake of the grace of God?

7. Why do people try to add things to grace rather than accept it?

8. How can you most effectively share God's grace with others?

Memory Verses

Titus 2:11–13

11   For the grace of God that bringeth salvation hath appeared to all men,

12   Teaching us that, denying ungodliness and worldly lusts, we should live soberly, righteously, and godly, in this present world;

13   Looking for that blessed hope, and the glorious appearing of the great God and our Saviour Jesus Christ;

A Relieving Grace

Text

1 KINGS 17:8–24

8   And the word of the LORD came unto him, saying,

9   Arise, get thee to Zarephath, which belongeth to Zidon, and dwell there: behold, I have commanded a widow woman there to sustain thee.

10   So he arose and went to Zarephath. And when he came to the gate of the city, behold, the widow woman was there gathering of sticks: and he called to her, and said, Fetch me, I pray thee, a little water in a vessel, that I may drink.

11   And as she was going to fetch it, he called to her, and said, Bring me, I pray thee, a morsel of bread in thine hand.

12   And she said, As the LORD thy God liveth, I have not a cake, but an handful of meal in a barrel, and a little oil in a cruse: and, behold, I am gathering two sticks, that I may go in and dress it for me and my son, that we may eat it, and die.

13   And Elijah said unto her, Fear not; go and do as thou hast said: but make me thereof a little cake first, and bring it unto me, and after make for thee and for thy son.

14   For thus saith the LORD God of Israel, The barrel of meal shall not waste, neither shall the cruse of oil fail, until the day that the Lord sendeth rain upon the earth.

15   And she went and did according to the saying of Elijah: and she, and he, and her house, did eat many days.

16   And the barrel of meal wasted not, neither did the cruse of oil fail, according to the word of the LORD, which he spake by Elijah.

17   And it came to pass after these things, that the son of the woman, the mistress of the house, fell sick; and his sickness was so sore, that there was no breath left in him.

18 *And she said unto Elijah, What have I to do with thee, O thou man of God? art thou come unto me to call my sin to remembrance, and to slay my son?*

19 *And he said unto her, Give me thy son. And he took him out of her bosom, and carried him up into a loft, where he abode, and laid him upon his own bed.*

20 *And he cried unto the LORD, and said, O LORD my God, hast thou also brought evil upon the widow with whom I sojourn, by slaying her son?*

21 *And he stretched himself upon the child three times, and cried unto the LORD, and said, O LORD my God, I pray thee, let this child's soul come into him again.*

22 *And the LORD heard the voice of Elijah; and the soul of the child came into him again, and he revived.*

23 *And Elijah took the child, and brought him down out of the chamber into the house, and delivered him unto his mother: and Elijah said, See, thy son liveth.*

24 *And the woman said to Elijah, Now by this I know that thou art a man of God, and that the word of the LORD in thy mouth is truth.*

Overview

Sometimes we think of grace only as a New Testament concept, but it is often seen in the Old Testament as well. In this Old Testament story, God demonstrates His grace in the life of the prophet Elijah. We see God's grace displayed in His provision not only for His prophet but also for the widow and her son.

We can be tempted to limit our thinking about grace to "church" matters, but it is for every need in life—physical, emotional, and spiritual. The relief that grace brings from the burdens and pressures we face cannot be found anywhere else: we must go to God to receive His grace during times of need.

Introduction

_____

_____

_____

I. The _____ of the Widow

1 KINGS 17:9–12

9 _Arise, get thee to Zarephath, which belongeth to Zidon, and dwell there: behold, I have commanded a widow woman there to sustain thee._

10 _So he arose and went to Zarephath. And when he came to the gate of the city, behold, the widow woman was there gathering of sticks: and he called to her, and said, Fetch me, I pray thee, a little water in a vessel, that I may drink._

11 _And as she was going to fetch it, he called to her, and said, Bring me, I pray thee, a morsel of bread in thine hand._

12 _And she said, As the Lord thy God liveth, I have not a cake, but an handful of meal in a barrel, and a little oil in a cruse: and, behold, I am gathering two sticks, that I may go in and dress it for me and my son, that we may eat it, and die._

PSALM 146:9

9 _The LORD preserveth the strangers; he relieveth the fatherless and widow: but the way of the wicked he turneth upside down._

A. _____

B. _____

JOB 36:15

15   *He delivereth the poor in his affliction, and openeth their ears in oppression.*

C. _____

II. The _____ of the Widow

1 KINGS 17:15

15   *And she went and did according to the saying of Elijah: and she, and he, and her house, did eat many days.*

A. *Faith to* _____

JOHN 11:40

40   *Jesus saith unto her, Said I not unto thee, that, if thou wouldest believe, thou shouldest see the glory of God?*

B. *Grace to* _____

1.   GRACE TO SERVE ELIJAH

PROVERBS 3:9–10

9   *Honour the LORD with thy substance, and with the firstfruits of all thine increase:*

10   *So shall thy barns be filled with plenty, and thy presses shall burst out with new wine.*

2.   GRACE TO GIVE TO ELIJAH

MARK 12:41–44

41   *And Jesus sat over against the treasury, and beheld how the people cast money into the treasury: and many that were rich cast in much.*

42 And there came a certain poor widow, and she threw in two mites, which make a farthing.

43 And he called unto him his disciples, and saith unto them, Verily I say unto you, That this poor widow hath cast more in, than all they which have cast into the treasury:

44 For all they did cast in of their abundance; but she of her want did cast in all that she had, even all her living.

2 CORINTHIANS 9:6–8

6 But this I say, He which soweth sparingly shall reap also sparingly; and he which soweth bountifully shall reap also bountifully.

7 Every man according as he purposeth in his heart, so let him give; not grudgingly, or of necessity: for God loveth a cheerful giver.

8 And God is able to make all grace abound toward you; that ye, always having all sufficiency in all things, may abound to every good work:

III. The _____ of the Widow

1 KINGS 17:16

16 And the barrel of meal wasted not, neither did the cruse of oil fail, according to the word of the LORD, which he spake by Elijah.

A. Grace _____ her physical need.

MATTHEW 9:28–29

28 And when he was come into the house, the blind men came to him: and Jesus saith unto them, Believe

ye that I am able to do this? They said unto him, Yea, Lord.

29   Then touched he their eyes, saying, According to your faith be it unto you.

B.   Grace _____ her fear.

1.   A TRAGIC LOSS

1 KINGS 17:17–18

17   And it came to pass after these things, that the son of the woman, the mistress of the house, fell sick; and his sickness was so sore, that there was no breath left in him.

18   And she said unto Elijah, What have I to do with thee, O thou man of God? art thou come unto me to call my sin to remembrance, and to slay my son?

2.   A TENDER PRAYER

1 KINGS 17:19–21

19   And he said unto her, Give me thy son. And he took him out of her bosom, and carried him up into a loft, where he abode, and laid him upon his own bed.

20   And he cried unto the LORD, and said, O LORD my God, hast thou also brought evil upon the widow with whom I sojourn, by slaying her son?

21   And he stretched himself upon the child three times, and cried unto the LORD, and said, O LORD my God, I pray thee, let this child's soul come into him again.

MATTHEW 21:22

22   And all things, whatsoever ye shall ask in prayer, believing, ye shall receive.

3.   A TRIUMPHANT RESURRECTION

1 KINGS 17:22–24

22   *And the LORD heard the voice of Elijah; and the soul of the child came into him again, and he revived.*
23   *And Elijah took the child, and brought him down out of the chamber into the house, and delivered him unto his mother: and Elijah said, See, thy son liveth.*
24   *And the woman said to Elijah, Now by this I know that thou art a man of God, and that the word of the LORD in thy mouth is truth.*

Conclusion

_____

_____

_____

Study Questions

1. What burdens was the widow in 1 Kings 17 carrying?

2. What burdens are you carrying today?

3. What burdens has grace helped you carry in the past?

4. How was the widow's faith demonstrated?

5. In what way did grace help the widow serve Elijah?

6. How did God's grace bless the widow?

7. How did the widow respond to the death of her son?

8. How has grace relieved a fear in your life?

Memory Verses

2 CORINTHIANS 9:6–8

6   But this I say, He which soweth sparingly shall reap also sparingly; and he which soweth bountifully shall reap also bountifully.

7   Every man according as he purposeth in his heart, so let him give; not grudgingly, or of necessity: for God loveth a cheerful giver.

8   And God is able to make all grace abound toward you; that ye, always having all sufficiency in all things, may abound to every good work:

A Rejoicing Grace

Text

COLOSSIANS 1:1–8

1 Paul, an apostle of Jesus Christ by the will of God, and Timotheus our brother,

2 To the saints and faithful brethren in Christ which are at Colosse: Grace be unto you, and peace, from God our Father and the Lord Jesus Christ.

3 We give thanks to God and the Father of our Lord Jesus Christ, praying always for you,

4 Since we heard of your faith in Christ Jesus, and of the love which ye have to all the saints,

5 For the hope which is laid up for you in heaven, whereof ye heard before in the word of the truth of the gospel;

6 Which is come unto you, as it is in all the world; and bringeth forth fruit, as it doth also in you, since the day ye heard of it, and knew the grace of God in truth:

7 As ye also learned of Epaphras our dear fellowservant, who is for you a faithful minister of Christ;

8 Who also declared unto us your love in the Spirit.

Overview

Grace changes everything. When God bestows grace on us, it transforms not only our eternal destiny but also the way we live and interact with others. As we look at Paul's letter to the church at Colosse, we can draw lessons about grace for our daily lives.

We'll look specifically at God's saving grace—what it is and then what it does.

Introduction

_____

_____

_____

COLOSSIANS 2:8–9

8 Beware lest any man spoil you through philosophy and vain deceit, after the tradition of men, after the rudiments of the world, and not after Christ.

9 For in him dwelleth all the fulness of the Godhead bodily.

I. The _____ of Saving Grace

A. Commences at _____ in Christ

EPHESIANS 2:8–9

8 For by grace are ye saved through faith; and that not of yourselves: it is the gift of God:

9 Not of works, lest any man should boast.

B. Continues throughout _____

1. IN A HEAVENLY HOME

JOHN 14:1–3

1 Let not your heart be troubled: ye believe in God, believe also in me.

2 In my Father's house are many mansions: if it were not so, I would have told you. I go to prepare a place for you.

3 And if I go and prepare a place for you, I will come again, and receive you unto myself; that where I am, there ye may be also.

2. FOR ALL WHO BELIEVE

2 THESSALONIANS 2:16

16   *Now our Lord Jesus Christ himself, and God, even our Father, which hath loved us, and hath given us everlasting consolation and good hope through grace.*

JOHN 1:17

17   *For the law was given by Moses, but grace and truth came by Jesus Christ.*

II. The _____ of Singing Grace

EPHESIANS 5:18–19

18   *And be not drunk with wine, wherein is excess; but be filled with the Spirit;*

19   *Speaking to yourselves in psalms and hymns and spiritual songs, singing and making melody in your heart to the Lord;*

A. *Because of a heart of _____*

COLOSSIANS 3:15–16

15   *And let the peace of God rule in your hearts, to the which also ye are called in one body; and be ye thankful.*

16   *Let the word of Christ dwell in you richly in all wisdom; teaching and admonishing one another in psalms and hymns and spiritual songs, singing with grace in your hearts to the Lord.*

B. *Because of a heart of _____*

2 CORINTHIANS 4:13–15

13   *We having the same spirit of faith, according as it is written, I believed, and therefore have I spoken; we also believe, and therefore speak;*

14 *Knowing that he which raised up the Lord Jesus shall raise up us also by Jesus, and shall present us with you.*

15 *For all things are for your sakes, that the abundant grace might through the thanksgiving of many redound to the glory of God.*

C. *Because of a heart filled with* _____
JOHN 5:39–40

39 *Search the scriptures; for in them ye think ye have eternal life: and they are they which testify of me.*

40 *And ye will not come to me, that ye might have life.*

III. The _____ of Speaking Grace
COLOSSIANS 4:3–6

3 *Withal praying also for us, that God would open unto us a door of utterance, to speak the mystery of Christ, for which I am also in bonds:*

4 *That I may make it manifest, as I ought to speak.*

5 *Walk in wisdom toward them that are without, redeeming the time.*

6 *Let your speech be alway with grace, seasoned with salt, that ye may know how ye ought to answer every man.*

A. *Grace to* _____ *the Gospel*
1 TIMOTHY 3:16

16 *And without controversy great is the mystery of godliness: God was manifest in the flesh, justified in the Spirit, seen of angels, preached unto the Gentiles, believed on in the world, received up into glory.*

1.   GOD PREPARED THE WAY.

2.   PAUL PREACHED THE WORD.
EPHESIANS 6:19–20
19 And for me, that utterance may be given unto me, that I may open my mouth boldly, to make known the mystery of the gospel,
20 For which I am an ambassador in bonds: that therein I may speak boldly, as I ought to speak.

B. *Grace to _____ others*
EPHESIANS 4:29
29 Let no corrupt communication proceed out of your mouth, but that which is good to the use of edifying, that it may minister grace unto the hearers.

Conclusion

_____

_____

_____

Study Questions

1.   How do we receive God's saving grace?

2.   How and when did you receive God's saving grace?

3.   What three kinds of music does the Bible talk about?

4.   What three things in our heart will make us singing Christians?

5.   What has God done for you that you would like to share with the class?

6.   In what two specific areas of speech do we need God's grace?

7.   What does the Bible mean when it talks about a "mystery"?

8.   Who have you shared the Gospel with recently and what was the result?

Memory Verses

EPHESIANS 5:18–19

18   And be not drunk with wine, wherein is excess; but be filled with the Spirit;

19   Speaking to yourselves in psalms and hymns and spiritual songs, singing and making melody in your heart to the Lord;

A Restraining Grace

Text

TITUS 2:11–15

11   For the grace of God that bringeth salvation hath appeared to all men,

12   Teaching us that, denying ungodliness and worldly lusts, we should live soberly, righteously, and godly, in this present world;

13   Looking for that blessed hope, and the glorious appearing of the great God and our Saviour Jesus Christ;

14   Who gave himself for us, that he might redeem us from all iniquity, and purify unto himself a peculiar people, zealous of good works.

15   These things speak, and exhort, and rebuke with all authority. Let no man despise thee.

Overview

Grace is one of the most misunderstood and mischaracterized doctrines in the Word of God. Many people deliberately misconstrue grace to mean that, when a person possesses grace, he has the right to do anything he chooses. But God's Word does not give the Christian a license to live an unrestrained life.

Grace does offer us many gifts, most importantly, of course, is our salvation. But grace also places guidelines on our lives by teaching us to deny ungodliness and worldly lusts so that we can live sober, righteous, and godly lives. And the goodness of grace gives us a certain hope and expectation for the future.

Introduction

_____

_____

_____

I. The _____ of Grace

A. Grace _____ salvation.

1. SALVATION IS THROUGH CHRIST.
1 PETER 2:24
24 *Who his own self bare our sins in his own body on the tree, that we, being dead to sins, should live unto righteousness: by whose stripes ye were healed.*

2. SALVATION ACCOMPANIES REDEMPTION.
ROMANS 3:24
24 *Being justified freely by his grace through the redemption that is in Christ Jesus:*

B. Grace _____ our salvation.

1. IT IS FOR ALL MEN.
JOHN 3:15–16
15 *That whosoever believeth in him should not perish, but have eternal life.*
16 *For God so loved the world, that he gave his only begotten Son, that whosoever believeth in him should not perish, but have everlasting life.*

JOHN 4:13–14

13 Jesus answered and said unto her, Whosoever drinketh of this water shall thirst again:

14 But whosoever drinketh of the water that I shall give him shall never thirst; but the water that I shall give him shall be in him a well of water springing up into everlasting life.

2. IT IS FREE FOR ALL MEN.

ROMANS 6:23

23 For the wages of sin is death; but the gift of God is eternal life through Jesus Christ our Lord.

II. The _____ of Grace

A. Guidance _____ from ungodliness

1. DENY UNGODLINESS.

2. DENY WORLDLY LUSTS.

GALATIANS 5:13

13 For, brethren, ye have been called unto liberty; only use not liberty for an occasion to the flesh, but by love serve one another.

ROMANS 5:20–6:2

20 Moreover the law entered, that the offence might abound. But where sin abounded, grace did much more abound:

21 That as sin hath reigned unto death, even so might grace reign through righteousness unto eternal life by Jesus Christ our Lord.

6:1 What shall we say then? Shall we continue in sin, that grace may abound?

2   God forbid. How shall we, that are dead to sin, live any longer therein?

B. Guidance _____ a sanctified life

1.   WE SHOULD LIVE SOBERLY.

2.   WE SHOULD LIVE RIGHTEOUSLY.

3.   WE SHOULD LIVE GODLY.

1 THESSALONIANS 1:9

9   For they themselves shew of us what manner of entering in we had unto you, and how ye turned to God from idols to serve the living and true God;

III. The _____ of Grace

A. We have an _____ of Christ.

1.   IT IS AN ANTICIPATED TIME.

2.   IT IS A HAPPY TIME.

1 THESSALONIANS 1:10

10   And to wait for his Son from heaven, whom he raised from the dead, even Jesus, which delivered us from the wrath to come.

1 JOHN 3:1–3

1   Behold, what manner of love the Father hath bestowed upon us, that we should be called the sons of God: therefore the world knoweth us not, because it knew him not.

2   Beloved, now are we the sons of God, and it doth not yet appear what we shall be: but we know that, when he shall appear, we shall be like him; for we shall see him as he is.

3   And every man that hath this hope in him purifieth himself, even as he is pure.

B. We will see the _____ of Christ.

PHILIPPIANS 2:9–11

9   Wherefore God also hath highly exalted him, and given him a name which is above every name:

10   That at the name of Jesus every knee should bow, of things in heaven, and things in earth, and things under the earth;

11   And that every tongue should confess that Jesus Christ is Lord, to the glory of God the Father.

1.   A GLORIOUS APPEARING

2.   A PERSONAL APPEARING

Conclusion

_____

_____

_____

Study Questions

1. What is the relationship between grace and salvation?

2. How did you personally experience the saving grace of God?

3. To whom is the gift of salvation offered?

4. What does God's grace guide us away from?

5. What does God's grace guide us toward?

6. In what area(s) has grace led you toward godly living?

7. How will the goodness of grace be demonstrated?

8. What prophetic events still need to occur before the Second Coming?

Memory Verses

1 JOHN 3:1–3

1   Behold, what manner of love the Father hath bestowed upon us, that we should be called the sons of God: therefore the world knoweth us not, because it knew him not.

2   Beloved, now are we the sons of God, and it doth not yet appear what we shall be: but we know that, when he shall appear, we shall be like him; for we shall see him as he is.

3   And every man that hath this hope in him purifieth himself, even as he is pure.

A Remembering Grace

Text

HEBREWS 12:14–16

14 Follow peace with all men, and holiness, without which no man shall see the Lord:

15 Looking diligently lest any man fail of the grace of God; lest any root of bitterness springing up trouble you, and thereby many be defiled;

16 Lest there be any fornicator, or profane person, as Esau, who for one morsel of meat sold his birthright.

Overview

Though a Christian can never lose his salvation, every Christian risks failing the grace of God. Forgetting the purpose and power of God's grace places us right in the path of this danger. Every May, our nation sets aside a special Memorial Day to remember those who have given their lives for our freedom. In this same way, we, as Christians, need to specifically and intentionally remember what God has done for us.

In this lesson, we will look at three specific areas of remembrance vital to the Christian life—forgiving, focusing, and fearing the Lord.

Introduction

_____

_____

_____

I. Remember to _____
HEBREWS 12:14
14 Follow peace with all men, and holiness, without which no man shall see the Lord:

A. Forgiveness pursues _____.
ROMANS 14:19
19 Let us therefore follow after the things which make for peace, and things wherewith one may edify another.

B. Forgiveness defeats _____.
HEBREWS 12:15–16
15 Looking diligently lest any man fail of the grace of God; lest any root of bitterness springing up trouble you, and thereby many be defiled;
16 Lest there be any fornicator, or profane person, as Esau, who for one morsel of meat sold his birthright.

1. LOOKING DILIGENTLY

2. OVERCOMING BITTERNESS
EPHESIANS 4:30–32
30 And grieve not the holy Spirit of God, whereby ye are sealed unto the day of redemption.

31 Let all bitterness, and wrath, and anger, and clamour, and evil speaking, be put away from you, with all malice:

32 And be ye kind one to another, tenderhearted, forgiving one another, even as God for Christ's sake hath forgiven you.

2 PETER 3:18

18 But grow in grace, and in the knowledge of our Lord and Saviour Jesus Christ. To him be glory both now and for ever. Amen.

PROVERBS 4:23

23 Keep thy heart with all diligence; for out of it are the issues of life.

MATTHEW 7:16–17

16 Ye shall know them by their fruits. Do men gather grapes of thorns, or figs of thistles?

17 Even so every good tree bringeth forth good fruit; but a corrupt tree bringeth forth evil fruit.

II. Remember to _____

HEBREWS 12:18, 22

18 For ye are not come unto the mount that might be touched, and that burned with fire, nor unto blackness, and darkness, and tempest,

22 But ye are come unto mount Sion, and unto the city of the living God, the heavenly Jerusalem, and to an innumerable company of angels,

A. Keep a _____ focus.

PSALM 48:1–3

1 Great is the LORD, and greatly to be praised in the city of our God, in the mountain of his holiness.

2 Beautiful for situation, the joy of the whole earth, is mount Zion, on the sides of the north, the city of the great King.

3 God is known in her palaces for a refuge.

REVELATION 3:12

12 Him that overcometh will I make a pillar in the temple of my God, and he shall go no more out: and I will write upon him the name of my God, and the name of the city of my God, which is new Jerusalem, which cometh down out of heaven from my God: and I will write upon him my new name.

REVELATION 21:2

2 And I John saw the holy city, new Jerusalem, coming down from God out of heaven, prepared as a bride adorned for her husband.

B. Keep a _____ focus.

HEBREWS 12:23–24

23 To the general assembly and church of the firstborn, which are written in heaven, and to God the Judge of all, and to the spirits of just men made perfect,

24 And to Jesus the mediator of the new covenant, and to the blood of sprinkling, that speaketh better things than that of Abel.

REVELATION 19:7

7 Let us be glad and rejoice, and give honour to him: for the marriage of the Lamb is come, and his wife hath made herself ready.

III. Remember to _____

HEBREWS 12:25–29

25 See that ye refuse not him that speaketh. For if they escaped not who refused him that spake on earth, much more shall not we escape, if we turn away from him that speaketh from heaven:

26 Whose voice then shook the earth: but now he hath promised, saying, Yet once more I shake not the earth only, but also heaven.

27 And this word, Yet once more, signifieth the removing of those things that are shaken, as of things that are made, that those things which cannot be shaken may remain.

28 Wherefore we receiving a kingdom which cannot be moved, let us have grace, whereby we may serve God acceptably with reverence and godly fear:

29 For our God is a consuming fire.

PSALM 89:7

7 God is greatly to be feared in the assembly of the saints, and to be had in reverence of all them that are about him.

A. _____ His voice.

HEBREWS 1:1–2

1 God, who at sundry times and in divers manners spake in time past unto the fathers by the prophets,

2 Hath in these last days spoken unto us by his Son, whom he hath appointed heir of all things, by whom also he made the worlds.

B. _____ *His commandments.*

2 CORINTHIANS 5:11
11 *Knowing therefore the terror of the Lord, we persuade men; but we are made manifest unto God; and I trust also are made manifest in your consciences.*

1 PETER 4:17–18
17 *For the time is come that judgment must begin at the house of God: and if it first begin at us, what shall the end be of them that obey not the gospel of God?*
18 *And if the righteous scarcely be saved, where shall the ungodly and the sinner appear?*

Conclusion

_____

_____

_____

Study Questions

1. How does remembering to forgive protect us from bitterness?

2. Why must we look diligently for bitterness in our lives?

3. What truth did we learn about the divergence of bitterness and grace?

4. Where is our focus supposed to be?

5. Besides Jesus, whom are you looking forward to seeing again in Heaven?

6. What does it mean to fear the Lord?

7. How do we demonstrate our fear of the Lord?

8.   What grace has God shown in your life that you would like to remember and share?

Memory Verses

HEBREWS 12:14–15

14 *Follow peace with all men, and holiness, without which no man shall see the Lord:*

15 *Looking diligently lest any man fail of the grace of God; lest any root of bitterness springing up trouble you, and thereby many be defiled;*

A Rewarding Grace

Text

ACTS 4:32–37

32 And the multitude of them that believed were of one heart and of one soul: neither said any of them that ought of the things which he possessed was his own; but they had all things common.

33 And with great power gave the apostles witness of the resurrection of the Lord Jesus: and great grace was upon them all.

34 Neither was there any among them that lacked: for as many as were possessors of lands or houses sold them, and brought the prices of the things that were sold,

35 And laid them down at the apostles' feet: and distribution was made unto every man according as he had need.

36 And Joses, who by the apostles was surnamed Barnabas, (which is, being interpreted, The son of consolation,) a Levite, and of the country of Cyprus,

37 Having land, sold it, and brought the money, and laid it at the apostles' feet.

Overview

The early church was characterized by the presence of God's Spirit and grace. "Great grace" was manifested in their relationships, their giving, and their witness. The reason the church is not impacting the world as it should is that we lack the grace we read about in this passage.

God bestowed grace upon this early church to do His work, and in turn, He blessed them for their faithful service. In this lesson, we will study three areas on which God showered His blessing—gracious spirits, generous stewardship, and great soulwinning.

Introduction

_____

_____

_____

ACTS 2:41
41 *Then they that gladly received his word were baptized: and the same day there were added unto them about three thousand souls.*

I.   Gracious in Their _____

A.   *They were of one _____.*

1.   THEY HAD FAITH IN CHRIST.

ACTS 4:10–12
10 *Be it known unto you all, and to all the people of Israel, that by the name of Jesus Christ of Nazareth, whom ye crucified, whom God raised from the dead, even by him doth this man stand here before you whole.*
11 *This is the stone which was set at nought of you builders, which is become the head of the corner.*
12 *Neither is there salvation in any other: for there is none other name under heaven given among men, whereby we must be saved.*

2.   THEY HAD FELLOWSHIP IN CHRIST.

ACTS 2:42
42 *And they continued stedfastly in the apostles' doctrine and fellowship, and in breaking of bread, and in prayers.*

B. They were of one _____.

1. THEY WERE ONE IN CHRIST.

JOHN 17:11

11   And now I am no more in the world, but these are in the world, and I come to thee. Holy Father, keep through thine own name those whom thou hast given me, that they may be one, as we are.

2. THEY WERE ONE FOR CHRIST.

ACTS 2:9–11

9   Parthians, and Medes, and Elamites, and the dwellers in Mesopotamia, and in Judaea, and Cappadocia, in Pontus, and Asia,

10   Phrygia, and Pamphylia, in Egypt, and in the parts of Libya about Cyrene, and strangers of Rome, Jews and proselytes,

11   Cretes and Arabians, we do hear them speak in our tongues the wonderful works of God.

C. They were of one _____.

1 SAMUEL 18:1

1   And it came to pass, when he had made an end of speaking unto Saul, that the soul of Jonathan was knit with the soul of David, and Jonathan loved him as his own soul.

II. Generous in Their _____

A. The believers were _____.

2 CORINTHIANS 8:7–9

7   Therefore, as ye abound in every thing, in faith, and utterance, and knowledge, and in all diligence,

and in your love to us, see that ye abound in this grace also.

8   I speak not by commandment, but by occasion of the forwardness of others, and to prove the sincerity of your love.

9   For ye know the grace of our Lord Jesus Christ, that, though he was rich, yet for your sakes he became poor, that ye through his poverty might be rich.

B. *The believers were* _____.

1 TIMOTHY 6:17–18

17   Charge them that are rich in this world, that they be not highminded, nor trust in uncertain riches, but in the living God, who giveth us richly all things to enjoy;

18   That they do good, that they be rich in good works, ready to distribute, willing to communicate;

III. Great in Their _____

A. _____ *witness*

1.   POWER IN THE MESSENGERS

ACTS 1:8

8   But ye shall receive power, after that the Holy Ghost is come upon you: and ye shall be witnesses unto me both in Jerusalem, and in all Judaea, and in Samaria, and unto the uttermost part of the earth.

1 THESSALONIANS 1:5

5   For our gospel came not unto you in word only, but also in power, and in the Holy Ghost, and in much assurance; as ye know what manner of men we were among you for your sake.

2. POWER IN THE MESSAGE
ROMANS 1:16
16 For I am not ashamed of the gospel of Christ: for it is the power of God unto salvation to every one that believeth; to the Jew first, and also to the Greek.

B. _____ *witness*

1. PROVEN BY THE RESURRECTION
1 CORINTHIANS 15:3–8
3 For I delivered unto you first of all that which I also received, how that Christ died for our sins according to the scriptures;
4 And that he was buried, and that he rose again the third day according to the scriptures:
5 And that he was seen of Cephas, then of the twelve:
6 After that, he was seen of above five hundred brethren at once; of whom the greater part remain unto this present, but some are fallen asleep.
7 After that, he was seen of James; then of all the apostles.
8 And last of all he was seen of me also, as of one born out of due time.

2. PROVEN BY CHANGED LIVES
JOHN 12:9–11
9 Much people of the Jews therefore knew that he was there: and they came not for Jesus' sake only, but that they might see Lazarus also, whom he had raised from the dead.

10   *But the chief priests consulted that they might put Lazarus also to death;*

11   *Because that by reason of him many of the Jews went away, and believed on Jesus.*

Conclusion

_____

_____

_____

Study Questions

1. What three elements demonstrated the presence of grace in the church at Jerusalem?

2. What is the relationship between doctrine and fellowship?

3. What evidences of unity have you seen in your church?

4. What two things demonstrated grace in the early church's giving?

5. What does the New Testament call giving?

6. What made the early church great in their soulwinning?

7. Can you share an example of when you have seen the power of the Gospel?

8. What changes in your life point to the power of the Gospel?

Memory Verses

ACTS 4:32–33

32 And the multitude of them that believed were of one heart and of one soul: neither said any of them that ought of the things which he possessed was his own; but they had all things common.

33 And with great power gave the apostles witness of the resurrection of the Lord Jesus: and great grace was upon them all.

A Reviving Grace

Text

JAMES 4:1–7

1   From whence come wars and fightings among you? come they not hence, even of your lusts that war in your members?

2   Ye lust, and have not: ye kill, and desire to have, and cannot obtain: ye fight and war, yet ye have not, because ye ask not.

3   Ye ask, and receive not, because ye ask amiss, that ye may consume it upon your lusts.

4   Ye adulterers and adulteresses, know ye not that the friendship of the world is enmity with God? whosoever therefore will be a friend of the world is the enemy of God.

5   Do ye think that the scripture saith in vain, The spirit that dwelleth in us lusteth to envy?

6   But he giveth more grace. Wherefore he saith, God resisteth the proud, but giveth grace unto the humble.

7   Submit yourselves therefore to God. Resist the devil, and he will flee from you.

Overview

Every Christian reaches a point where he needs revival in his heart. The world, the flesh, and the devil are constantly working to lure our hearts away from full devotion to God. The sweetness of close fellowship with God that we once enjoyed can be lost a little at a time, almost without our realizing it. In this lesson we are going to examine what revival is, what hinders us from experiencing revival, how it comes to the people of God, and what the results of a genuine revival will be. By presenting the Bible model of revival, we will also equip our students to discern the allurements that draw some people away from the Lord.

Introduction

_____

_____

_____

I. The _____ with Revival

JAMES 3:14–16

14   But if ye have bitter envying and strife in your hearts, glory not, and lie not against the truth.

15   This wisdom descendeth not from above, but is earthly, sensual, devilish.

16   For where envying and strife is, there is confusion and every evil work.

A. *Conflict with* _____

PSALM 133:1

1   Behold, how good and how pleasant it is for brethren to dwell together in unity!

1. FIGHTING IN THE FLESH

2. NOT WALKING IN THE SPIRIT

GALATIANS 5:16–18

16   This I say then, Walk in the Spirit, and ye shall not fulfill the lust of the flesh.

17   For the flesh lusteth against the Spirit, and the Spirit against the flesh: and these are contrary the one to the other: so that ye cannot do the things that ye would.

18   *But if ye be led of the Spirit, ye are not under the law.*

B.   *Conflict with* _____

2 PETER 2:10

10   *But chiefly them that walk after the flesh in the lust of uncleanness, and despise government. Presumptuous are they, selfwilled, they are not afraid to speak evil of dignities.*

1.   THE PROCESS OF SELFISHNESS

2.   THE PRODUCT OF SELFISHNESS

2 PETER 2:17–21

17   *These are wells without water, clouds that are carried with a tempest; to whom the mist of darkness is reserved for ever.*

18   *For when they speak great swelling words of vanity, they allure through the lusts of the flesh, through much wantonness, those that were clean escaped from them who live in error.*

19   *While they promise them liberty, they themselves are the servants of corruption: for of whom a man is overcome, of the same is he brought in bondage.*

20   *For if after they have escaped the pollutions of the world through the knowledge of the Lord and Saviour Jesus Christ, they are again entangled therein, and overcome, the latter end is worse with them than the beginning.*

21   *For it had been better for them not to have known the way of righteousness, than, after they have known it, to turn from the holy commandment delivered unto them.*

II. The _____ for Revival

A. Misplaced _____

B. Misplaced _____

1 JOHN 2:15–16

15 Love not the world, neither the things that are in the world. If any man love the world, the love of the Father is not in him.

16 For all that is in the world, the lust of the flesh, and the lust of the eyes, and the pride of life, is not of the Father, but is of the world.

1 PETER 1:18–19

18 Forasmuch as ye know that ye were not redeemed with corruptible things, as silver and gold, from your vain conversation received by tradition from your fathers;

19 But with the precious blood of Christ, as of a lamb without blemish and without spot:

2 CORINTHIANS 11:1–3

1 Would to God ye could bear with me a little in my folly: and indeed bear with me.

2 For I am jealous over you with godly jealousy: for I have espoused you to one husband, that I may present you as a chaste virgin to Christ.

3 But I fear, lest by any means, as the serpent beguiled Eve through his subtilty, so your minds should be corrupted from the simplicity that is in Christ.

COLOSSIANS 2:8

8 Beware lest any man spoil you through philosophy and vain deceit, after the tradition of men, after the rudiments of the world, and not after Christ.

C. *Misplaced* _____

III. The _____ of Revival

A. *Revival begins with a* _____ *heart.*
PSALM 51:10
10   *Create in me a clean heart, O God; and renew a right spirit within me.*

JAMES 4:10
10   *Humble yourselves in the sight of the Lord, and he shall lift you up.*

B. *Revival develops a* _____ *heart.*

1.   A HUMBLE HEART SUBMITS TO GOD'S LEADING.

2.   A HUMBLE HEART RESISTS THE DEVIL.

Conclusion

_____

_____

_____

REVELATION 3:19–20
19   *As many as I love, I rebuke and chasten: be zealous therefore, and repent.*
20   *Behold, I stand at the door, and knock: if any man hear my voice, and open the door, I will come in to him, and will sup with him, and he with me.*

Study Questions

1. What are the conflicts that attempt to block revival from our lives?

2. How does selfishness manifest itself in the life of a Christian?

3. What can selfishness kill in our lives?

4. What things can compete with revival for our attention?

5. To what does God compare the process of our hearts being drawn away from Him?

6. How are you striving to be a friend of sinners without being a friend of the world?

7. What relationship does revival have with the condition of our hearts?

8. What does God do when our hearts are proud instead of humble?

Memory Verses

1 JOHN 2:15–16

15 *Love not the world, neither the things that are in the world. If any man love the world, the love of the Father is not in him.*

16 *For all that is in the world, the lust of the flesh, and the lust of the eyes, and the pride of life, is not of the Father, but is of the world.*

A Reassuring Grace

Text

2 TIMOTHY 1:5–9

5   When I call to remembrance the unfeigned faith that is in thee, which dwelt first in thy grandmother Lois, and thy mother Eunice; and I am persuaded that in thee also.

6   Wherefore I put thee in remembrance that thou stir up the gift of God, which is in thee by the putting on of my hands.

7   For God hath not given us the spirit of fear; but of power, and of love, and of a sound mind.

8   Be not thou therefore ashamed of the testimony of our Lord, nor of me his prisoner: but be thou partaker of the afflictions of the gospel according to the power of God;

9   Who hath saved us, and called us with an holy calling, not according to our works, but according to his own purpose and grace, which was given us in Christ Jesus before the world began,

Overview

We are living in a world of uncertainty and doubt. Many people are struggling with the pressures and fears they face to the point that some of the best-selling prescription drugs in America are depression and anxiety treatments. But God has the best answer for His children—He offers us His grace.

In this lesson, we will study the role that grace plays in giving us assurance and confidence during difficult times. We will look at the promise of God to provide us with power, love, and a sound mind. The same grace that helped the Apostle Paul through great persecution, suffering, and even martyrdom is available to us today.

Introduction

_____

_____

_____

I. His Grace Reassures Us with _____

A. *Power from the* _____

1. THE HOLY SPIRIT RESIDES IN EVERY BORN-AGAIN CHRISTIAN.

JOHN 3:6
6   *That which is born of the flesh is flesh; and that which is born of the Spirit is spirit.*

ROMANS 8:8–9
8   *So then they that are in the flesh cannot please God.*
9   *But ye are not in the flesh, but in the Spirit, if so be that the Spirit of God dwell in you. Now if any man have not the Spirit of Christ, he is none of his.*

2. THE HOLY SPIRIT IMPARTS GRACE AND STRENGTH TO A YIELDED CHRISTIAN.

LUKE 24:49
49   *And, behold, I send the promise of my Father upon you: but tarry ye in the city of Jerusalem, until ye be endued with the power from on high.*

1 THESSALONIANS 5:19
19   *Quench not the Spirit.*

B. *Power for every* _____

1. POWER FOR WITNESSING

1 THESSALONIANS 1:5

5   For our gospel came not unto you in word only, but also in power, and in the Holy Ghost, and in much assurance; as ye know what manner of men we were among you for your sake.

2. POWER IN PERSECUTION

COLOSSIANS 1:10–11

10   That ye might walk worthy of the Lord unto all pleasing, being fruitful in every good work, and increasing in the knowledge of God;

11   Strengthened with all might, according to his glorious power, unto all patience and longsuffering with joyfulness;

ROMANS 8:26

26   Likewise the Spirit also helpeth our infirmities: for we know not what we should pray for as we ought: but the Spirit itself maketh intercession for us with groanings that cannot be uttered.

II. His Grace Reassures Us with _____

A. *A love for* _____

1. WE RESPOND TO HIS LOVE.

1 JOHN 4:19

19   We love him, because he first loved us.

2. WE REFLECT THE SPIRIT OF HIS LOVE.

1 JOHN 4:18

18   There is no fear in love; but perfect love casteth out fear: because fear hath torment. He that feareth is not made perfect in love.

B. A love for _____

GALATIANS 5:22

22   But the fruit of the Spirit is love…

GALATIANS 5:25

25   If we live in the Spirit, let us also walk in the Spirit.

III. His Grace Reassures Us with a

_____

A. Through _____

1. SALVATION IS AVAILABLE THROUGH JESUS CHRIST.

TITUS 3:4–7

4   But after that the kindness and love of God our Saviour toward man appeared,

5   Not by works of righteousness which we have done, but according to his mercy he saved us, by the washing of regeneration, and renewing of the Holy Ghost;

6   Which he shed on us abundantly through Jesus Christ our Saviour;

7   That being justified by his grace, we should be made heirs according to the hope of eternal life.

2. SALVATION ALLOWS US THE ABILITY TO
   UNDERSTAND SPIRITUAL THINGS.

1 CORINTHIANS 2:14

*14   But the natural man receiveth not the things
of the Spirit of God: for they are foolishness unto
him: neither can he know them, because they are
spiritually discerned.*

B. *Through the* _____

1. THE SCRIPTURES GIVE WISDOM.

2 TIMOTHY 3:15

*15   And that from a child thou hast known the holy
scriptures, which are able to make thee wise unto
salvation through faith which is in Christ Jesus.*

PROVERBS 1:7

*7   The fear of the LORD is the beginning of knowledge:
but fools despise wisdom and instruction.*

2. THE SCRIPTURES PRODUCE A SOUND MIND.

2 TIMOTHY 3:16–17

*16   All scripture is given by inspiration of God, and is
profitable for doctrine, for reproof, for correction, for
instruction in righteousness:*

*17   That the man of God may be perfect, throughly
furnished unto all good works.*

C. *Through the* _____ *of Jesus Christ*

1 THESSALONIANS 4:13–18

*13   But I would not have you to be ignorant, brethren,
concerning them which are asleep, that ye sorrow not,
even as others which have no hope.*

14   For if we believe that Jesus died and rose again, even so them also which sleep in Jesus will God bring with him.

15   For this we say unto you by the word of the Lord, that we which are alive and remain unto the coming of the Lord shall not prevent them which are asleep.

16   For the Lord himself shall descend from heaven with a shout, with the voice of the archangel, and with the trump of God: and the dead in Christ shall rise first.

17   Then we which are alive and remain shall be caught up together with them in the clouds, to meet the Lord in the air: and so shall we ever be with the Lord.

18   Wherefore comfort one another with these words.

Conclusion

_____

_____

_____

Study Questions

1. How does God's grace reassure us with power?

2. How has God empowered you to be an effective witness for Him?

3. How does God's grace reassure us with love?

4. What are we doing when we show love to others?

5. What does it mean to have a sound mind?

6. What fears can keep you from having a sound mind?

7. How does God's grace reassure us with a sound mind?

8. How were we called to be God's children?

Memory Verses

COLOSSIANS 1:10–11

10 *That ye might walk worthy of the Lord unto all pleasing, being fruitful in every good work, and increasing in the knowledge of God;*

11 *Strengthened with all might, according to his glorious power, unto all patience and longsuffering with joyfulness.*

A Reinforcing Grace

Text

ROMANS 5:1–5

1 *Therefore being justified by faith, we have peace with God through our Lord Jesus Christ:*

2 *By whom also we have access by faith into this grace wherein we stand, and rejoice in hope of the glory of God.*

3 *And not only so, but we glory in tribulations also: knowing that tribulation worketh patience;*

4 *And patience, experience; and experience, hope:*

5 *And hope maketh not ashamed; because the love of God is shed abroad in our hearts by the Holy Ghost which is given unto us.*

Overview

When a general is planning a battle, one of his most important strategies is positioning his troops so there will be reinforcements available if something goes wrong in one area of the battle. If he cannot provide help at the crucial moment, the entire battle may be lost.

The Christian life is a life of spiritual warfare. We are wrestling in a life-and-death struggle against a very real enemy committed to our destruction. But we have reinforcements available to us. Grace provides the help we need to fight and win the battles we face. In this lesson we're going to study how grace supplies what we lack in the areas of unity, stability, and maturity. With these missing elements supplied, we are prepared for every attack of the enemy.

Introduction

_____

_____

_____

I. A Grace That Brings _____

A. _____ comes through justification.
Romans 3:23
23 For all have sinned, and come short of the glory of God.

1. THE MEANING OF JUSTIFICATION

2. THE MESSAGE OF JUSTIFICATION
Romans 5:10
10 For if, when we were enemies, we were reconciled to God by the death of his Son, we shall be saved by his life.

B. Justification is the _____ of the Lord Jesus.

1. HE SATISFIED GOD'S JUST DEMANDS.
Romans 3:24–26
24 Being justified freely by his grace through the redemption that is in Christ Jesus:
25 Whom God hath set forth to be a propitiation through faith in his blood, to declare his righteousness for the remission of sins that are past, through the forbearance of God;

26 *To declare, I say, at this time his righteousness: that he might be just, and the justifier of him which believeth in Jesus.*

2. HE RECONCILED MAN TO GOD.

EPHESIANS 1:6–7

6 *To the praise of the glory of his grace, wherein he hath made us accepted in the beloved.*

7 *In whom we have redemption through his blood, the forgiveness of sins, according to the riches of his grace;*

EPHESIANS 2:15–16

15 *Having abolished in his flesh the enmity, even the law of commandments contained in ordinances; for to make in himself of twain one new man, so making peace;*

16 *And that he might reconcile both unto God in one body by the cross, having slain the enmity thereby:*

II. A Grace That Brings _____

1 PETER 5:10–11

10 *But the God of all grace, who hath called us unto his eternal glory by Christ Jesus, after that ye have suffered a while, make you perfect, stablish, strengthen, settle you.*

11 *To him be glory and dominion for ever and ever. Amen.*

A. *His grace is _____.*

HEBREWS 10:19–23

19 *Having therefore, brethren, boldness to enter into the holiest by the blood of Jesus,*

20 *By a new and living way, which he hath consecrated for us, through the veil, that is to say, his flesh;*

21 *And having an high priest over the house of God;*

22 *Let us draw near with a true heart in full assurance of faith, having our hearts sprinkled from an evil conscience, and our bodies washed with pure water.*

23 *Let us hold fast the profession of our faith without wavering; (for he is faithful that promised;)*

HEBREWS 4:14–16

14 *Seeing then that we have a great high priest, that is passed into the heavens, Jesus the Son of God, let us hold fast our profession.*

15 *For we have not an high priest which cannot be touched with the feeling of our infirmities; but was in all points tempted like as we are, yet without sin.*

16 *Let us therefore come boldly unto the throne of grace, that we may obtain mercy, and find grace to help in time of need.*

B. *His grace is* _____.

C. *His grace brings* _____.

TITUS 3:5–7

5 *Not by works of righteousness which we have done, but according to his mercy he saved us, by the washing of regeneration, and renewing of the Holy Ghost;*

6 *Which he shed on us abundantly through Jesus Christ our Saviour;*

7 *That being justified by his grace, we should be made heirs according to the hope of eternal life.*

1 PETER 1:3–4

3   *Blessed be the God and Father of our Lord Jesus Christ, which according to his abundant mercy hath begotten us again unto a lively hope by the resurrection of Jesus Christ from the dead,*

4   *To an inheritance incorruptible, and undefiled, and that fadeth not away, reserved in heaven for you,*

ROMANS 8:31–39

31   *What shall we then say to these things? If God be for us, who can be against us?*

32   *He that spared not his own Son, but delivered him up for us all, how shall he not with him also freely give us all things?*

33   *Who shall lay anything to the charge of God's elect? It is God that justifieth.*

34   *Who is he that condemneth? It is Christ that died, yea rather, that is risen again, who is even at the right hand of God, who also maketh intercession for us.*

35   *Who shall separate us from the love of Christ? shall tribulation, or distress, or persecution, or famine, or nakedness, or peril, or sword?*

36   *As it is written, For thy sake we are killed all the day long; we are accounted as sheep for the slaughter.*

37   *Nay, in all these things we are more than conquerors through him that loved us.*

38   *For I am persuaded, that neither death, nor life, nor angels, nor principalities, nor powers, nor things present, nor things to come,*

39   *Nor height, nor depth, nor any other creature, shall be able to separate us from the love of God, which is in Christ Jesus our Lord.*

III. A Grace That Brings _____

A. *Maturity through* _____

B. *Maturity to bring* _____
   JAMES 1:2–4
   2   My brethren, count it all joy when ye fall into divers temptations;
   3   Knowing this, that the trying of your faith worketh patience.
   4   But let patience have her perfect work, that ye may be perfect and entire, wanting nothing.

C. *Maturity through* _____

D. *Maturity to* _____

Conclusion

_____

_____

_____

Study Questions

1. How does grace work to bring us unity?

2. What did Jesus do for us on the Cross?

3. How has grace produced unity in your life?

4. How does grace bring stability to our lives?

5. What is something that you hoped for in the past that God made a reality for you?

6. What is something you are trusting and hoping for God to do in your life?

7. In what four ways does grace produce maturity in our lives?

8. What is the biblical meaning of hope?

Memory Verses

HEBREWS 4:14–16

14   Seeing then that we have a great high priest, that is passed into the heavens, Jesus the Son of God, let us hold fast our profession.

15   For we have not an high priest which cannot be touched with the feeling of our infirmities; but was in all points tempted like as we are, yet without sin.

16   Let us therefore come boldly unto the throne of grace, that we may obtain mercy, and find grace to help in time of need.

Striving Together
P u b l i c a t i o n s

For additional Christian
growth resources visit
www.strivingtogether.com